# I eat a rainbow

## Bobbie Kalman

 Crabtree Publishing Company

www.crabtreebooks.com

# Created by Bobbie Kalman

**Author and Editor-in-Chief**
Bobbie Kalman

**Educational consultants**
Reagan Miller
Elaine Hurst
Joan King

**Editors**
Joan King
Reagan Miller
Kathy Middleton

**Proofreader**
Crystal Sikkens

**Photo research**
Bobbie Kalman

**Design**
Bobbie Kalman
Katherine Berti

**Print and production coordinator**
Katherine Berti

**Prepress technician**
Katherine Berti

**Photographs**
iStockphoto: cover (fruits and vegetables), p. 1, 13 (children)
Shutterstock: cover (children), p. 1, 3 (except apple, banana,
and orange), 4, 5 (except apple, bananas, and orange), 6,
7, 8, 9, 10, 11, 12, 13 (except children), 14 (except lemon
and tomato), 15 (except carrots, peas, and strawberries),
16 (bottom)
Other photos by Comstock and Photodisc

Library and Archives Canada Cataloguing in Publication

Kalman, Bobbie, 1947-
    I eat a rainbow / Bobbie Kalman.

(My world)
ISBN 978-0-7787-9412-7 (bound).--ISBN 978-0-7787-9456-1 (pbk.)

    1. Food--Juvenile literature.  2. Nutrition--Juvenile
literature.  3. Colors--Juvenile literature.
I. Title.  II. Series: My world (St. Catharines, Ont.).

TX355.K343 2010          j613.2          C2009-906047-7

Library of Congress Cataloging-in-Publication Data

Kalman, Bobbie.
    I eat a rainbow / Bobbie Kalman.
        p. cm. --  (My world)
    ISBN 978-0-7787-9412-7 (reinforced lib. bdg. : alk. paper) --
    ISBN 978-0-7787-9456-1 (pbk. : alk. paper)
    1. Nutrition--Juvenile literature.  I. Title.

    RA784.K25 2010
    613.2--dc22

                                          2009040950

## Crabtree Publishing Company

www.crabtreebooks.com          1-800-387-7650

Printed in Canada / 062021 / MA20210603

**Published in Canada**
**Crabtree Publishing**
616 Welland Ave.
St. Catharines, Ontario
L2M 5V6

**Published in the United States**
**Crabtree Publishing**
347 Fifth Ave
Suite 1402-145
New York, NY 10016

**Published in the United Kingdom**
**Crabtree Publishing**
Maritime House
Basin Road North, Hove
BN41 1WR

**Published in Australia**
**Crabtree Publishing**
Unit 3-5
Currumbin Court
Capalaba QLD 4157

# Words to know

banana

blueberry

apple

orange

child

cherry

pepper

rainbow

red

orange

yellow

green

blue

purple

A rainbow has these colors.

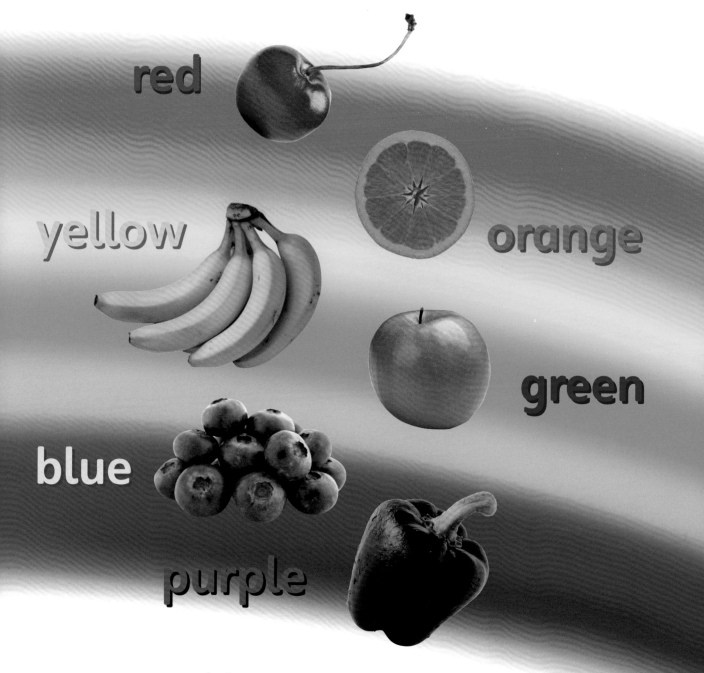

red

yellow

orange

green

blue

purple

Food has rainbow colors.

cherry

The cherry is red.

orange

The orange is orange.

banana

The banana is yellow.

apple

The apple is green.

blueberry

The blueberry is blue.

pepper

The pepper is purple.

I eat a rainbow every day.

orange

red

yellow

purple

green

blue

I am a rainbow child.

## Activity

Which foods are red?

Which foods are orange?

Which foods are yellow?

Which foods are green?

Which foods are blue?

Which foods are purple?

corn

lemon

grapes

tomato

14

peas

plums

strawberry

carrots

pumpkin

peppers

# Notes for adults

## Eating naturally

*I eat a rainbow* introduces children to the healthful habit of eating natural foods of every color, every day. Nutritionists have discovered that we need foods of different colors to boost our immune systems, moderate our moods, and help our brains function better. Fruits such as apples, bananas, blueberries, red grapes, cherries, and oranges, and vegetables such as peppers, dark leafy greens, broccoli, tomatoes—and many more rainbow foods provide the body with important nutrients and fiber. This book can lead to a child's awareness that natural foods are what his or her body needs to function well and feel good.

## Energy and colors from the sun

A rainbow is the sun's light broken into colors. You could show children how light breaks into rainbow colors by shining light through a prism.

Our energy also comes from the sun. This energy moves from the sun through the food chain and into our bodies when we eat. Introducing the concept of energy from the sun will help children understand that eating a "rainbow" of colorful foods gives them all the energy and nutrients they need to keep healthy. That's why they are "rainbow kids!"

*More advanced readers will love* ***What color is it?*** *This fun book shows examples of rainbow colors in nature—in red-eyed tree frogs, orange butterflies and tigers, and blue-footed boobies.*
***Guided Reading: I***

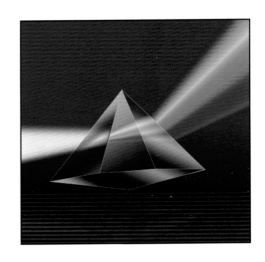